# Balancing The THIN Blue Line

Inspirational Quotes to Help Balance Being a Police Officer and Your Personal Life

Copyright © 2015 CURT THOMAS UNLIMITED, LLC

All rights reserved. No part of this book may be reproduced or transmitted in any form or by any means, electronic or mechanical, including photocopying, recording, or by any information storage and retrieval system, without permission in writing from the copyright owner.

ISBN: 978-0-9961977-4-8

Library of Congress Control Number: 2015904213

CURT THOMAS UNLIMITED, LLC Mount Pleasant, SC

# Dedication

This book is dedicated to "South Carolina's Finest", The South Carolina Highway Patrol. I'm grateful to have served with you for nearly seven years. From the Colonel down to the newest trooper, I have learned something from each of you. To my family at Troop 7 Post B... "Drive on S.I.R." Thank You!

To the surrounding agencies that has help me become a "decent" trooper. Orangeburg Department of Public Safety, Orangeburg County Sheriff's Office, Santee Police Department, Cameron Police Department, Eutawville Police Department, St. Matthews Police Department, Calhoun County Sheriff's Office, Springfield Police Department, North Police Department, Branchville Police Department, Holly Hill Police Department, Elloree Police Department, Claflin University Public Safety, South Carolina State University Police Department, The Regional Medical Center Security, The Department of Natural Resources, SLED, The South Carolina Department of Public Safety, South Carolina

State Transportation Police, The South Carolina Criminal Justice Academy, The South Carolina Trooper's Association, The South Carolina Law Enforcement Network(SCLEN), The South Carolina Bureau of Protective Services, The South Carolina Probation & Parole, The South Carolina Forestry Commission, The Orangeburg County Detention Center and Judges and their staff at Orangeburg and

Calhoun Municipalities and Magistrates offices, and the brave Firefighters and EMS personal in Orangeburg/ Calhoun County... Thank you...

To all my law enforcement brothers and sisters worldwide... Many people don't understand what you do on a day-to-day basis. This book is to encourage you doing good days and the not so good days. Thank you for what you do...

Finally, my favorite dispatchers at the South Carolina Department of Public Safety! Thank you for keeping me safe over the years! Thank you!

May this book help you "Balance the THIN Blue Line"

God Bless...

Curt, SCHP "2389"

This quotes book is designed to be inspirational and motivational for the reader.

It is designed for you to read and re-read from time to time.

The hope of the author is for your consciousness to grow to reveal a different interpretation each time you read a quote in this book. Whether it's every day or once a week, motivation and inspiration is continual.

# Quotes for the PROFESSION

"Never disrespect your dispatcher! It could be the difference between you getting dispatched to a legitimate call or being sent to the furthest point in your jurisdiction for an 'anonymous call'."

— Curt Thomas

"People sleep peaceably in their beds at night only because rough men stand ready to do violence on their behalf."

— George Orwell

"All men/women are not created equal. The finest become policemen/women!"

— Curt Thomas

"Courage is the most important of all the virtues because without courage, you can't practice any other virtue consistently."

— Maya Angelou

"To handle yourself, use your head; to handle others, use your heart."

— Eleanor Roosevelt

"Leadership is about being a servant first."

— Allen West

"If you ever want to know when it's time for promotions for the Sergeant position and above, start looking for simple 'write ups' around the office."

— Curt Thomas

"Motivation is what gets you started. Habit is what keeps you going."

— Jim Ryun

"Leaders must be close enough to relate to others, but far enough ahead to motivate them."

— John C. Maxwell

"Courage is found in unlikely places."

— J.R.R. Tolkien

"Staying BALANCED as an officer is vital."

— Curt Thomas

"Without continual growth and progress, such words as improvement, achievement, and success have no meaning."

— Benjamin Franklin

"Courage is not the absence of fear, but rather the judgement that something else is more important than fear."

— Ambrose Redmoon

"Most police officers that I knew or worked with, wore four "shirt stays" just to look GOOD, I wore six of them to look EXCELLENT! Two TV commercials later..."

— Curt Thomas

"If I have to come back over here again for the same shit (call), then 'lottie dottie' I'm locking up every MF body!"

— Unknown

"Coming together is a beginning; keeping together is progress; working together is success."

— Henry Ford

"If you're walking down the right path and you're willing to keep walking, eventually you'll make progress."

— President Barack Obama

"Don't be afraid of your fears. They're not there to scare you. They're there to let you know that something is worth it."

— C. JoyBell C.

"I always stayed humbled as a state trooper. I loved working with other agencies.
I didn't care if they were from the city, county or a damn security officer, if I needed help, I just wanted to see blue lights coming to help. I think the worse thing an officer can have is the 'I'm better than you' attitude.
We all look the same to a bullet from a criminal's gun."

— Curt Thomas

"Blessed are the peacemakers: for they shall be called the children of God."


— Matthew 5:9

"Confront the dark parts of yourself, and work to banish them with illumination and forgiveness. Your willingness to wrestle with your demons will cause your angels to sing."

— August Wilson

"Every time someone would say to me, 'I could NEVER do your job', I would just smile and say to them, 'you're right'."

— Curt Thomas

"If there is no enemy within, the enemy outside can do you no harm."

— African Proverb

"Nothing ever comes to one that is worth having, except as a result of hard work."

— Booker T. Washington

"Without fear there cannot be courage."

— Christopher Paolini

"If you hate cops the next time you need help, call a criminal."


— Unknown

"He who rejects change is the architect of decay. The only human institution which rejects progress is the cemetery."

— Harold Wilson

"Freedom lies in being bold."

— Robert Frost

"Treat everyone like a million dollars but have a plan in the back of your head to kill them if you have to..."

— Unknown

"I worked for the highway patrol for nearly 7 years. I pressed my patrol uniform 95% of the time.
The other 5% was when we 'had' a budget for dry cleaning."

— Curt Thomas

"People run from crimes such as shootings, fights, domestic violence, terrorist attacks, vehicle accidents...police officers run to it!"

— Unknown

"If you are filled with pride, then you will have no room for wisdom."

— African proverb

"There are three kinds of people in the world. There are wolves and there are sheep. And then there are those who protect the sheep from the wolves."

— Christopher Shields

"You can always tell when stress is getting to someone in charge; they will go from smoking a ½ pack of cigarettes to 2 packs a day and lose 10- 15lbs in a month."

— Curt Thomas

"The best executive is the one who has sense enough to pick good men to do what he wants done, and self-restraint to keep from meddling with them while they do it."

—Theodore Roosevelt

"I learned that courage was not the absence of fear, but the triumph over it. The brave man is not he who does not feel afraid, but he who conquers that fear."

— Nelson Mandela

"No amount of law enforcement can solve a problem that goes back to the family."

— J. Edgar Hoover

"Trying to have the 'SUPERMAN mentality' when dealing with people will get you killed quicker than anything else as a police officer. When in doubt call for backup. At least you will live to talk about it!"

— Curt Thomas

"Learn to ask for help,
not because you're weak
but because you want to
remain strong."

— Unknown

"I never competed against another officers with stats. My goal was to always serve each customer (people I encounter) with the best representation of myself and my organization. To make necessary arrests, be there for my partners when they needed help, then take my ass home! The community won't remember your 'competition' when you're dead, but they will remember the service you rendered."

— Curt Thomas

"You don't know how fast you were going? I guess that means I can write anything I want to on the ticket, huh?"

— Unknown

"Leadership is not about titles, positions, or flow charts. It is about one life influencing another."

— John C. Maxwell

"Courage isn't having the strength to go on - it is going on when you don't have strength."

— Napoléon Bonaparte

"No mam, we don't have a quota to meet each month. If we did you would get another ticket for those bald tires you're driving on and those 1970 windshield wiper blades."

— Curt Thomas

"If you run, you'll only go to jail tired."


— Unknown

> "In God we trust; all others we run through NCIC."
> (National Crime Identification Center)
>
> — Unknown

"You didn't think we give pretty women tickets? You're right, we don't… Here's your ticket, sign here."

— Unknown

"Always watch your 6!"

— Unknown

"No, you're WRONG. I'm even TOUGHER without the badge and gun."


— Unknown

"I never really invited many of my co-workers to my home. Having one gun in the house was more than enough."

— Curt Thomas

"No matter how long you train someone to be brave, you never know if they are or not until something real happens."

— Veronica Roth

"We all have had that 'dream' when you wrecked your patrol car on the way to a call or the dream where you're in a gun fight and you're trying to shoot back but your gun jammed, or you are about get shot. It's really hard to explain to anyone else other than a brother or sister in blue."

— Curt Thomas

"Yes, sir, you can talk to the shift supervisor, but I don't think it will help. Oh, did I mention that I'm the shift supervisor?"

— Unknown

"Courage is being scared to death but saddling up anyway."

— John Wayne

"People may hear your words, but they feel your attitude."

— John C. Maxwell

"When I was a state trooper, I look at each officer as my brothers and sisters. I would take a bullet for them and any other police officer in a heartbeat! That's just a bond we all shared."

— Curt Thomas

"Don't tell people how to do things, tell them what to do and let them surprise you with their results."

—George Patton

"We cannot be sure of having something to live for unless we are willing to die for it."

— Che Guevara

"Trust me, you don't do this job for the money. If you looking to just make money, there's always a position open at Burger King for that."

— Curt Thomas

"Never neglect details. When everyone's mind is dulled or distracted the leader must be doubly vigilant."

— Colin Powell

"Take advantage of every opportunity to practice your communication skills so that when important occasions arise, you will have the gift, the style, the sharpness, the clarity, and the emotions to affect other people."

—Jim Rohn

"There's nothing worse than seeing a dirty ass patrol car then seeing a police officer step out the car with a wrinkled uniform and his shift is just beginning! Some of us still take pride with our appearance and our office (the patrol car)."

— Curt Thomas

"Do not forget what is to be a sailor because of being a captain yourself."

— Tanzanian proverb

"It is not sacrifice if you love what you're doing."

— Mia Hamm

"Sometimes when I think my personal problems are too much to handle, the next call (dispatched) reminds me that maybe my problems aren't that bad after all."

— Curt Thomas

"No matter how good you are at planning, the pressure never goes away. So, I don't fight it. I feed off it. I turn pressure into motivation to do my best."

— Benjamin Carson

"True strength is keeping everything together when everyone expects you to fall apart."

— Unknown

"Carelessness is worse than a thieve."

— Scottish Proverb

"Police officers deal with the same problems other people deal with but they still put their life on the line for the safety of others."

— Curt Thomas

"All the great things are simple, and many can be expressed in a single word: freedom, justice, honor, duty, mercy, hope."

— Winston Churchill

"The precinct secretary is the one who is really in charge of the department. Better stay on his or her good side."

— Curt Thomas

"Management is doing things right; leadership is doing the right things."

— Peter F. Drucker

"There is a special place in heaven for good police officers. For the one or two that didn't make it...there's a special place for them too."


— Curt Thomas

"Thank you, Father, for giving me the grace to do this job (police officer). Without you, I don't know what I'm doing...but with you I can do all things. I pray for courage in the midst of a crisis, faith in the mist of fear. I pray I don't have to pull my weapon out against my enemy but if I do, I pray I end it with one shot to the head or center mass. I pray for my safety and the safety of my co- workers and my family at home from danger seen and unseen. Thank you for hearing my prayer. Let's go!"

— Curt Thomas

-My prayer before EVERY shift and a simple 'thank you for keeping me safe' at the end of watch.

# Quotes for Personal Life

"When you get off work from patrol and turn the ignition off to go into your home to be with your family, the stress of your day wants to follow you inside. Leave it in the car.
You family wants to feel you not the stress from your day."

— Curt Thomas

"Wink at small faults, for you have great ones yourself."

— Scottish Proverb

"Optimism is the faith that leads to achievement. Nothing can be done without hope and confidence."


— Helen Keller

"Every officer needs to have a 'relief valve' from the stress of being a police officer. Fishing, golfing, hunting, basketball, baseball, watching movies with the kids, etc. Without a 'relief valve', we fall quickly into depression, alcoholism, financial trouble, divorce, or even suicidal thoughts. I know, I've been there...luckily, I'm still here. Balance is important."

—Curt Thomas

"Every day begins with an act of courage and hope: getting out of bed."

— Mason Cooley

"It takes one person to forgive; it takes two people to be reunited."

— Lewis B. Smedes

"The day before I shot my first television commercial for DUI crackdown, my electricity was <u>turned off</u>. I knew it would be off when I got home. So, I ironed my uniform a day before just so it would be <u>pressed</u> for the camera. I ran water in the tub just so I could bathe the next day. I had to charge my cell phone in my patrol car just so I wouldn't oversleep. I went to the patrol office early the next morning to shave then headed to the shoot. I gave it <u>100%</u> during the shoot despite my circumstance. I felt my state deserved to see nothing less than 100% while watching me represent South Carolina's Finest. I know the struggle of making ends meet while on a policeman's salary and going through a divorce but it's a calling."

— Curt Thomas

"Love begins by taking care of the closest ones - the ones at home."

— Mother Teresa

"In times of great stress or adversity, it's always best to keep busy, to plow your anger and your energy into something positive."

— Lee Iacocca

"The time you feel lonely is
the time you most need to
be by yourself."


— Douglas Coupland

"Take care of your body. It's the only place you have to live."

— Jim Rohn

"What gives me the most hope every day is God's grace; knowing that his grace is going to give me the strength for whatever I face, knowing that nothing is a surprise to God."

— Rick Warren

"Family is not an important thing. It's everything."

— Michael J. Fox

"Life is funny. Things change, people change, but you will always be you, so stay true to yourself and never sacrifice who you are for anyone."

— Zayn Malik

"No family is perfect... we argue, we fight. We even stop talking to each other at times. But in the end, family is family... The love will always be there."

— Unknown

"Staying **BALANCED** as an officer is vital."

— Curt Thomas

"Good actions give strength to ourselves and inspire good actions in others."

— Plato

"If your wife or husband was there for your before you became a police officer, don't become a bad-ass overnight! He or she deserves that respect. I learned this the hard way."

— Curt Thomas

"Live so that when your children think of fairness, caring, and integrity, they think of you."


— H. Jackson Brown, Jr.

"Let us sacrifice our today so that our children can have a better tomorrow."

— A. P. J. Abdul Kalam

"The love of family and the admiration of friends is much more important than wealth and privilege."

— Charles Kuralt

"I got so many counselling sessions about my reports being turned in late. I never intended for them to be late...ever! Seeing my kids and wife so happy to see me back home safe and alive from shift, caused me to temporarily forget about the report. Yep, I'll take that counselling session."

— Curt Thomas

"Depression isn't about, 'Woe is me, my life is this, that and the other', it's like having the worst flu all day that you just can't kick."

— Robbie Williams

"That which does not kill us makes us stronger."

— Friedrich Nietzsche

"Take time to spend with your kids and family. You never know when your 'watch' will end."

— Curt Thomas

"Peace is a journey of a thousand miles and it must be taken one step at a time."

— Lyndon B. Johnson

"Kids of police officers are the coolest kids in the entire school. Who wants to mess with a kid whose mom or dad carries a gun and handcuffs?"

— Curt Thomas

"My biggest hobby is hanging out with my family and kids."

— Joel Osteen

"When your kids stop talking to you and your wife or husband stop greeting you at the door when you get home from work, they are quietly asking for your time."


— Curt Thomas

"Be not afraid of growing slowly, be afraid only of standing still."

— Chinese Proverb

"Life is lived on the edge."

— Will Smith

"Most officers secretly suffer from depression, anxiety attacks at home, anger problems, alcoholism, loneliness, and frustrations. Yet we will still suit up to serve and protect. Most people could never understand that kind of life."

— Curt Thomas

"To handle yourself, use your head; to handle others, use your heart."

— Eleanor Roosevelt

"While in law enforcement, I went through a divorce. It was very dangerous to be working on the dangerous streets <u>and</u> emotionally drained. I could have easily gotten killed. Most of us won't go to therapy because of pride but it's better to get it off our chest verses holding it all inside."

— Curt Thomas

"The ache for home lives in all of us, the safe place where we can go as we are and not be questioned."

— Maya Angelou

"The best way to cheer yourself up is to try to cheer somebody else up."

— Mark Twain

"Thinking of my children got me through many tough shifts. Thinking of them during the difficult days made it worth it."

— Curt Thomas

"You will not be punished for your anger; you will be punished by your anger."

— Buddha

"A little more persistence, a little more effort, and what seemed hopeless failure may turn to glorious success."

— Elbert Hubbard

"Learn to say 'no' to the good so you can say 'yes' to the best."

— John C. Maxwell

"I am as bad as the worst, but, thank God, I am as good as the best."

— Walt Whitman

"The minute you raise your hands to strike your child or wife (husband) the way you would strike violator, it's best to ask for some time off to spend with your family or see a chaplain as soon as possible. Being proactive costs you nothing but trying to explain after you hurt someone will cost you everything!"

— Curt Thomas

"The only way to keep your health is to eat what you don't want, drink what you don't like, and do what you'd rather not."

— Mark Twain

"You can never be passed up for a promotion. Someone in a higher position will always remember you character. Focus on maintaining your character and a better position will be yours."

— Curt Thomas

"The best use of life is love. The best expression of love is time. The best time to love is now."

— Rick Warren

"All of us have the possibility of <u>not</u> making it home when we leave home for work. Value the time with family while you are alive."

— Curt Thomas

"When anger rises, think of the consequences."

— Confucius

"Faith is taking the first step even when you don't see the whole staircase."

— Martin Luther King, Jr.

"Family is the most important thing in the world."

— Princess Diana

"Get more involved in the community. They don't bite.

— Curt Thomas

"Happiness doesn't depend on any external conditions; it is governed by our mental attitude."

— Dale Carnegie

"Learn to ask for help,
not because you're weak
but because you want to
remain strong."


— Unknown

"Having a spiritual relationship with the Supreme Being has kept me through so many rough times in my life. It's EVERYTHING to me."

— Curt Thomas

"No matter how good you are at planning, the pressure never goes away. So, I don't fight it. I feed off it. I turn pressure into motivation to do my best."

— Benjamin Carson

"The weak can never forgive. Forgiveness is the attribute of the strong."


— Mahatma Gandhi

"If you can dream it, you can do it."

— Walt Disney

"The more I see the less I know for sure."

— John Lennon

"Thank you, Father, for giving me the grace to do this job (police officer). Without you, I don't know what I'm doing... but with you I can do all things. I pray for courage in the midst of a crisis, faith in the mist of fear. I pray I don't have to pull my weapon out against my enemy but if I do, I pray I end it with one shot to the head or center mass. I pray for my safety and the safety of my co- workers and my family at home from danger seen and unseen. Thank you for hearing my prayer. Let's go!"

— Curt Thomas

-

- My prayer before EVERY shift and a simple 'thank you for keeping me safe' after the end of watch.

Thank you for protecting and serving the community, county, state, and our nation

I hope this book will help you stay motivated to do what you do...during those good days and those not so good days!

They world is a better place because of what you do!

Stay safe out there...

Your Brother,

Curt

Website: www.thecurtthomas.com

For bulk orders or request Curt to speak at your department or law enforcement conference, email us at:

info@thecurtthomas.com